THREE LITTLE PIGS

The oldest pig comes home from work every 4 days. The middle one comes home every 3 days, and the youngest comes home every 2 days. If they are all leaving today, how many more days will it be until all the pigs are home together again?

Answer on page 48

Hint on page 46

The answer for each problem is on a tourist's shirt, bag, or other item. Can you send each visitor to the right rest spot?

SHUTTLE

$0 + 2$

$22 \div 2$

$2 \div 2$

$1 + 2$

$(2 \times 2) \times (2 + 1)$

2×3

Illustration: Scott Peck

Answer on page 48

STACKING STANLEY

Stanley was stacking some cartons when he noticed something funny. He could find the numbers on some of the boxes by adding the numbers on the two cartons directly below each one. When he finished stacking, he was ready to write in the missing numbers so that the numbers in the entire pyramid worked in this way. Can you beat him to it?

STAN

55

27

11

7

4   2

Answer on page 48

Illustration: B/Michael Polan

PIÑATA PUZZLER

The piñata just broke open. Can you figure out how many of the 11 partygoers got a turn to break the piñata before it came apart?

Illustration: John Nez

Hint on page 46

Ariel got a turn and so did Courtney.

Brett didn't get a turn and neither did Darrice.

Eleanor hit the piñata only once.

Francisco was the child who broke the piñata.

Geraldo went after Herman, but before Ignacio.

Herman's turn came right after Eleanor.

Jamie was to go after Francisco, but before Kiandra.

Answer on page 48

A FISH TALE

Charlie loves tropical fish. He told so many relatives that he wanted a fishbowl for his birthday that he got three of them! He received several fish

UP TO 6 MONTHS OLD

6 MONTHS TO 1 YEAR OLD

8

in each bowl, and so he decided to split them up. Read the clues, then draw each fish in its proper bowl.

Hint on page 46

FISH

Goldy—Very round, dark orange, $\frac{6}{5}$ years old

Spot—Orange with one black spot, $\frac{11}{12}$ year old

Tiny—Small pink fish with big black eyes, $\frac{1}{3}$ year old

Finley—Yellow with big blue fins, $\frac{1}{8}$ year old

Blubber—Big, light orange, $\frac{5}{8}$ year old

Aqua—Blue with purple spots, $\frac{3}{5}$ year old

Big Red—Red with a black stripe and small eyes, $\frac{3}{10}$ year old

Ray—Flat with a pointy tail, $\frac{9}{7}$ years old

Pesce—Silver with big wispy tail, $\frac{6}{8}$ year old

Zeebee—Black-and-white stripes, $\frac{3}{2}$ years old

Illustration: Rick Geary

OLDER THAN 1 YEAR

Tropica FISH FOOD

ZIP IT

66804	66804	66804
33021	89212	33021
43666	66804	43666
	43666	

You should zip through this in no time. If everyone in the same small town has the same ZIP code, which ZIP codes belong on which envelopes?

Illustration: Terry Rogers

1. Joe Kerr
23 Skiddoo Street
Hilltown, MI

7. Doug Dubs
222 Two Street
Centerville, FL

8. Honey Bee
22 Bumble Lane, Apt. 4B
Hilltown, MI

4. Marv L. Us
7 Wonderful Way
Lake City, OH

2. Wanda A. Bout
313 Roam Road
Hilltown, MI

9. P. Ano
88 Keys Drive
Lake City, OH

5. Dee Tectiff
15 Mystery Mile
Huron, CA

3. Willie Duit
1 Neverknows Street
Huron, CA

10. Rose Tulips
44 Bouquet Drive
Lake City, OH

6. Oscar Tony
56 Grammy Way
Hilltown, MI

Answer on page 48

DOTS A LOT

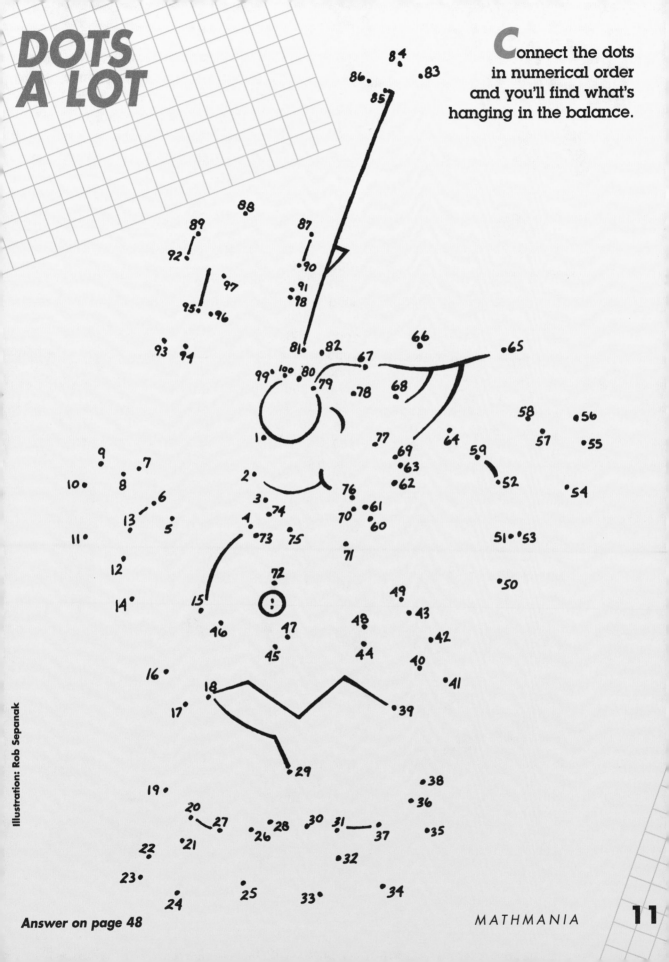

Illustration: Rob Sepanak

MATHMANIA **11**

ALL NEW DEPTHS

This puzzle is really deep. That's because it features some of the world's deepest lakes. To find these depths, solve the problem beside each lake. (A lake is a body of water surrounded by land. Although some lakes are called seas, they are still lakes.)

LAKE (continent)	DEPTH	
Baykal (Asia)	5000 + 300 + 10 + 5	_____
Tanganyika (Africa)	4000 + 800 + 20 + 3	_____
Caspian Sea (Asia)	3000 + 300 + 60 + 3	_____
Issyk Kul (Asia)	2000 + 300 + 3	_____
Nyasa (Africa)	2000 + 200 + 80	_____
Great Slave (North America)	2000 + 10 + 5	_____
Great Bear (North America)	1000 + 400 + 60 + 3	_____
Superior (North America)	1000 + 300 + 30	_____
Michigan (North America)	900 + 20 + 3	_____
Titicaca (South America)	900 + 20 + 2	_____
Ontario (North America)	800 + 2	_____
Huron (North America)	700 + 50	_____
Ladoga (Europe)	700 + 30 + 8	_____
Reindeer (North America)	700 + 20	_____
Athabasca (North America)	400 + 7	_____
Kariba (Africa)	300 + 90	_____
Aral Sea (Asia)	200 + 20	_____
Erie (North America)	200 + 10	_____
Maracaibo (South America)	100 + 10 + 5	_____
Balkhash (Asia)	80 + 5	_____

Once you have the numbers, dive down to the grid. Look up, down, across, backward, or diagonally to find the answers. Many numbers will appear in more than one answer. To match our answer, all the numbers will be used at least once.

```
5 9 0 7 0 4
0 1 2 9 8 2
5 7 1 2 3 5
1 3 3 0 8 1
3 0 3 8 4 0
5 2 6 6 5 2
9 7 3 7 8 2
```

Illustration: Bradley Clark

Hint
on
page
46

RIVER RUN

Each kayaker is taking a different river to Camp Acorn, and each is paddling at a different speed. Can you tell the order in which they will arrive at camp?

RED RIVER

YELLOW RIVER

WHITE RIVER

GREEN RIVER

Hint on page 46

Illustration: Bill Colrus

RIVERS	LENGTH	KAYAKERS	SPEED
White	42 miles	Noel	7 mph
Red	30 miles	Olivia	6 mph
Yellow	44 miles	Pablo	11 mph
Green	24 miles	Qan	8 mph

Answer on page 49

FAMOUS NAME

If you connect the dots in the order listed, you will find the name of the person described in this autobiography.

Illustration: Kit Wray

I was born a slave in the early 19th century. My original name was Araminta Ross. I escaped slavery in 1849 and went to Philadelphia. During the Civil War, I acted as a spy for the Union Army. I became a leader of the Underground Railroad movement and personally helped to free hundreds of slaves. I led so many north to freedom that my own people called me Moses.

```
    A B C D E F G H I J K L M N O
1   . . . . . . . . . . . . . . .
2   . . . . . . . . . . . . . . .
3   . . . . . . . . . . . . . . .
4   . . . . . . . . . . . . . . .
5   . . . . . . . . . . . . . . .
6   . . . . . . . . . . . . . . .
```

A1-A3	B1-B3	C1-C3	D1-D3	E1-E3	F1-F2	G1-G3
H1-H2	I1-I3	J1-J3	M1-M3	B4-B6	D4-D6	E4-E6
F4-F6	G4-G6	H4-H6	J4-J6	K4-K6	L4-L6	M4-M6
O4-O6	C1-D1	E1-F1	G1-H1	J1-K1	L1-N1	A4-C4
F4-G4	K4-L4	A2-B2	C2-D2	E2-F2	G2-H2	J2-K2
F5-G5	K5-L5	J3-K3	D6-E6	F6-G6	E2-F3	G2-H3
H4-I5	J4-I5	M4-O6				

DOMINO THEORY

In a full set of dominoes, each of the 28 tiles has two halves. Domino halves with the same number of dots are placed next to each other. For instance, a 4 is placed next to a 4, a 3 is placed next to a 3, and so on. A tile placed with its middle crosswise against another tile has an equal number of dots on each side. Can you place the tiles in the correct spots on the board to the right? We've used circles on the finished board to represent those halves that have no dots. The tiles with Xs are already in position on the board.

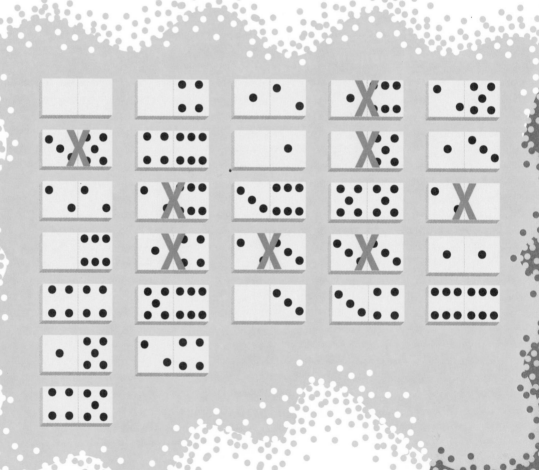

Hint on page 46

Answer on page 49

DIGIT DOES IT

Though it's not really his field, that intrepid investigator, Inspector Digit, knows good vegetables. He'd been stalking a corn crook for weeks when

he came upon this latest crime scene. The only clue that was left behind was a note. Can you decipher it and help the Inspector gather the clues?

Answer on page 49

$\overline{10}\ \overline{8}\ \overline{5}\ \overline{7}$ $\overline{22}\ \overline{1}\ \overline{16}\ \overline{11}\ \overline{8}\ \overline{18}\ \overline{12}\ \overline{21}\ \overline{7}$ $\overline{10}\ \overline{22}\ \overline{2}\ \overline{22}\ \overline{12}$ '

$\overline{5}\ \overline{13}$ ' $\overline{16}\ \overline{9}\ \overline{19}\ \overline{18}\ \overline{3}\ \overline{16}$! $\overline{12}\ \overline{9}\ \overline{22}\ \overline{16}$

$\overline{16}\ \overline{21}\ \overline{19}\ \overline{1}\ \overline{10}\ \overline{16}$ $\overline{18}\ \overline{21}\ \overline{7}\ \overline{1}\ \overline{4}$ ' $\overline{15}\ \overline{19}\ \overline{12}$ $\overline{22}$

$\overline{16}\ \overline{9}\ \overline{21}\ \overline{19}\ \overline{20}\ \overline{10}$ $\overline{9}\ \overline{5}\ \overline{6}\ \overline{8}$ $\overline{20}\ \overline{22}\ \overline{16}\ \overline{12}\ \overline{8}\ \overline{1}\ \overline{8}\ \overline{10}$

$\overline{13}\ \overline{9}\ \overline{8}\ \overline{1}$ $\overline{22}$ $\overline{13}\ \overline{5}\ \overline{16}$ $\overline{22}\ \overline{1}$ $\overline{12}\ \overline{9}\ \overline{8}$

$\overline{18}\ \overline{7}\ \overline{22}\ \overline{15}$. $\overline{17}\ \overline{4}$ $\overline{11}\ \overline{21}\ \overline{11}$ $\overline{16}\ \overline{5}\ \overline{22}\ \overline{10}$ $\overline{12}\ \overline{21}$

$\overline{3}\ \overline{8}\ \overline{8}\ \overline{11}$ $\overline{17}\ \overline{4}$ $\overline{8}\ \overline{5}\ \overline{7}\ \overline{16}$ $\overline{21}\ \overline{11}\ \overline{8}\ \overline{1}$ $\overline{5}\ \overline{1}\ \overline{10}$

$\overline{16}\ \overline{12}\ \overline{5}\ \overline{4}$ $\overline{5}\ \overline{13}\ \overline{5}\ \overline{4}$ $\overline{14}\ \overline{7}\ \overline{21}\ \overline{17}$ $\overline{18}\ \overline{7}\ \overline{22}\ \overline{17}\ \overline{8}$.

$\overline{22}\ \overline{12}\ \overline{16}$, $\overline{12}\ \overline{22}\ \overline{17}\ \overline{8}$ $\overline{12}\ \overline{21}$ $\overline{18}\ \overline{5}\ \overline{16}\ \overline{9}$

$\overline{22}\ \overline{1}$ $\overline{17}\ \overline{4}$ $\overline{18}\ \overline{9}\ \overline{22}\ \overline{11}\ \overline{16}$ $\overline{5}\ \overline{1}\ \overline{10}$ $\overline{13}\ \overline{22}\ \overline{16}\ \overline{9}$

$\overline{17}\ \overline{4}\ \overline{16}\ \overline{8}\ \overline{20}\ \overline{14}$ $\overline{22}\ \overline{1}\ \overline{12}\ \overline{21}$ $\overline{12}\ \overline{9}\ \overline{8}$

$\overline{18}\ \overline{21}\ \overline{7}\ \overline{1}\ \overline{14}\ \overline{22}\ \overline{8}\ \overline{20}\ \overline{10}$. $\overline{2}\ \overline{21}\ \overline{21}\ \overline{10}$ $\overline{20}\ \overline{19}\ \overline{18}\ \overline{3}$

$\overline{18}\ \overline{20}\ \overline{8}\ \overline{5}\ \overline{1}\ \overline{22}\ \overline{1}\ \overline{2}$ $\overline{21}\ \overline{19}\ \overline{12}$ $\overline{5}\ \overline{20}\ \overline{20}$

$\overline{G}\ \overline{N}$ $\overline{8}\ \overline{5}\ \overline{7}\ \overline{16}$!

$\overline{7}\ \overline{21}\ \overline{15}$ $\overline{18}\ \overline{21}\ \overline{15}\ \overline{15}$

Illustration: Joe Boddy

Hint on page 46

TILE TOTAL

50

56

62

64

70

72

78

80

Answer on page 49

SALE!

Hint on page 47

Illustration: Ron Zalme

MARKET PICKS

Dana went to the Merry Market and purchased half of the items on her shopping list. She spent exactly $11.22. Can you tell which four items she bought?

SHOPPING LIST

soap $2.29
magazine $3.50
batteries $4.19
vitamins $5.64
bottled water $1.40
box of tissues $1.89
shower curtain . . . $9.95
new mop $7.86

Hint on page 47

Illustration: Rocky Fuller

Answer on page 49

SCRAMBLED PICTURE

Copy these mixed-up rectangles onto the next page to unscramble the scene.

A-3   A-2   A-1   A-4

B-2   B-4   B-3   B-1

C-4   C-3   C-1   C-2

D-3   D-2   D-4   D-1

The letters and numbers tell
you where each rectangle
belongs. We've done the first
one, A-3, to start you off.

	1	2	3	4
A				
B				
C				
D				

Answer on page 49

NUMBER NOODLER

Can you figure out which number is hiding here?

Hint on page 47

1. The number is not larger than 50.
2. The number does not contain two digits that are the same.
3. The number does not divide evenly by 5.
4. The number does not contain any even digits.
5. The number is not smaller than 20.
6. The number does not contain the digit 1.
7. The sum of the two digits of the number is not 12.

Illustration: Beth Griffis Johnson

Answer on page 49

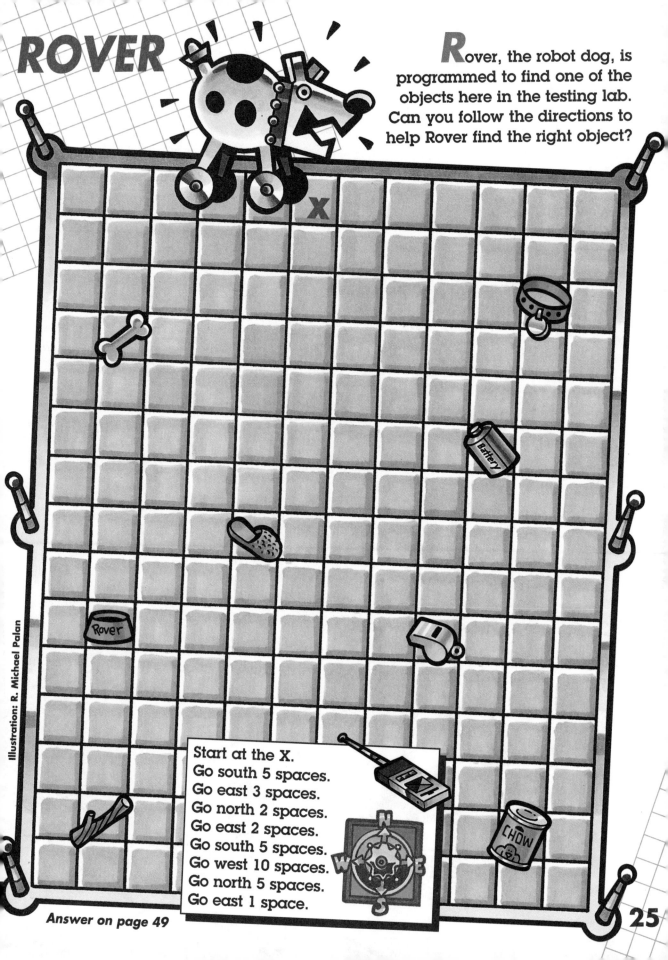

ROVER

Rover, the robot dog, is programmed to find one of the objects here in the testing lab. Can you follow the directions to help Rover find the right object?

Start at the X.
Go south 5 spaces.
Go east 3 spaces.
Go north 2 spaces.
Go east 2 spaces.
Go south 5 spaces.
Go west 10 spaces.
Go north 5 spaces.
Go east 1 space.

Illustration: R. Michael Palan

Answer on page 49

CROSSWORD RIDDLE

Fill in these boxes with the letters of the words that answer each clue or description. When you've completed the grid, rearrange the letters in the yellow and blue boxes to discover the answer to our riddle.

ACROSS

1. Million, billion, _____
5. Santa __, New Mexico
6. Abbreviation for *Rhode Island*
8. Number of musketeers on a candy bar
11. Dollar bills with less value than tens or fives
13. Four letters on a compass in this order: bottom, top, left, right
15. Number of octopus arms
17. Abbreviation for *television*
18. How a sailor might say *yes*
20. One dozen plus two

DOWN

1. Place for a king or queen to sit
2. "One __ by land . . ."
3. Contraction of *let us*
4. Number of wheels on a unicycle
7. Opposite of *out*
9. What you do in a marathon
10. Roman numeral XI
12. What a chicken contributes to an omelet
13. Short for *statistic*
14. Abbreviation for *weight*
16. The usual answer to the questions in a wedding ceremony
19. Old English for *you*

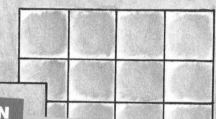

Hint on page 47

Answer on page 50

They always make your day:

▢ ▢ ▢ ▢ ▢ ▢ - ▢ ▢ ▢ ▢

▨ ▨ ▨ ▨ ▨ .

27

SURE SHOTS

Jessica practices her free throws every day. She gives herself 5 points for every basket and takes off 2 points for every miss. If she took 12 shots and scored 32 points, how many baskets did she make?

Illustration: Joe Boddy

Answer on page 50

BRAINTEASER

A.

$$0 + 1 + 2 + 3 + 4 + 5 =$$

B.

$$0 \times 1 \times 2 \times 3 \times 4 \times 5 =$$

Illustration: Jerry Zimmerman

Answer on page 50

MYSTERIOUS MINUTES

Someone ate Ali Gator's submarine sandwich! At precisely 7:00 p.m., she went onstage to sing her new hit, "Swimming in the Rain." She was away from her dressing table for exactly 9 minutes.

Hint on page 47

Answer on page 50

The five other entertainers in the club are the only ones who had keys to the dressing room. Use the clues to help the club manager figure out who ate the sandwich.

SUSPECTS

L. E. Fant was playing the piano for Anna Conda while she practiced her four songs. They started at 6:30, and each song took exactly 11 minutes.

Ty Gerr spent 10 minutes doing his vocal scales and took another 10 minutes practicing his song "I Howl a Happy Tune." He began 19 minutes after Anna Conda started.

Bill Frogg finished practicing his cello 30 minutes before Robyn Bird finished.

Robyn Bird practiced her violin 15 minutes more after L. E. Fant stopped playing the piano, but she started 9 minutes later.

MATHMAGIC

Pick a number from 2 to 9. It can be 2 or 9 or any number in between.

Multiply that number by 9.

That should give you a two-digit number. Take those two digits and add them together.

Take the resulting number and subtract 5 from it.

Take that number and match it to the alphabet, numbering the letters (A = 1, B = 2, C = 3, and so on).

Take your letter and think of a country that begins with that letter.

Take the last letter in the name of that country and think of an animal.

Now, take the last letter in the name of that animal and think of a color.

I have a message for you on page 50.

Illustration: Marc Nadel

PRECISE ICE

Re-create this image without crossing over any lines or removing your pencil from the page.

Illustration: Barbara Gray

Answer on page 50

TOUCHDOWN TIME

This game has been a tough one. Look at the six attempts to score. Using the field,

SHARKS

1. Started on their own 40-yard line
   1st play: gained 20 yards
   2nd play: lost 10 yards
   3rd play: gained 15 yards
   4th play: gained 7 yards

2. Started on their own 30-yard line
   1st play: gained 10 yards
   2nd play: gained 10 yards
   3rd play: gained 20 yards
   4th play: gained 32 yards

3. Started on the Hornets' 40-yard line
   1st play: gained 10 yards
   2nd play: lost 20 yards
   3rd play: gained 30 yards
   4th play: gained 22 yards

HORNETS

1. Started on the 50-yard line
   1st play: lost 16 yards
   2nd play: gained 25 yards
   3rd play: gained 15 yards
   4th play: gained 15 yards

2. Started on their own 30-yard line
   1st play: lost 5 yards
   2nd play: gained 45 yards
   3rd play: gained 10 yards
   4th play: gained 10 yards

3. Started on their own 40-yard line
   1st play: gained 10 yards
   2nd play: gained 20 yards
   3rd play: gained 10 yards
   4th play: gained 21 yards

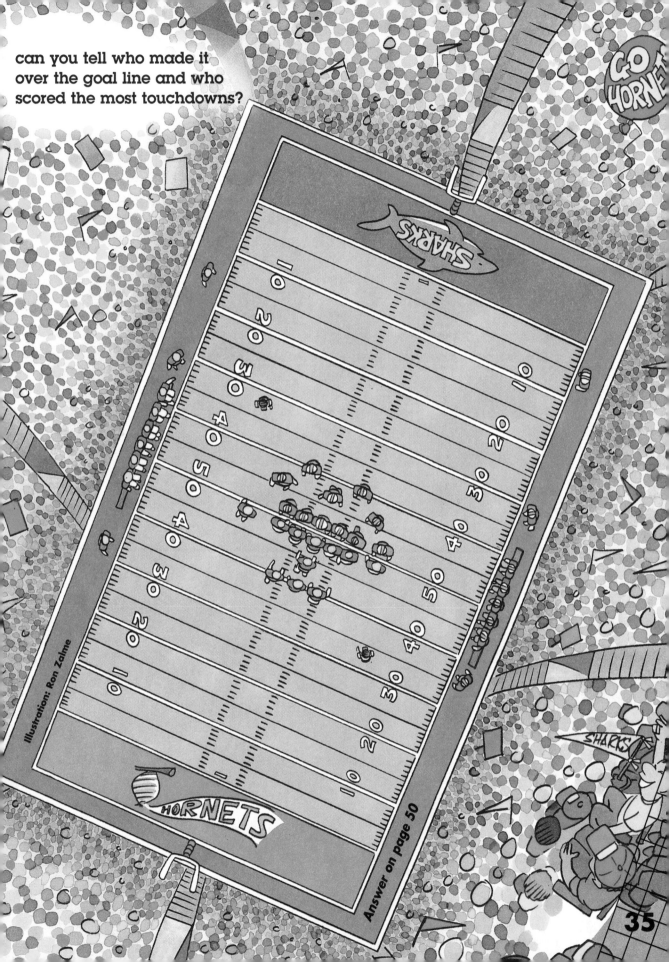

LIBRARY LAUGHS

Dewey has some funny books in his library. To check one out, solve each problem. Then go to the shelves to find the volume with the number that matches each answer. Put the matching letter in the blank beside each answer. Read down the letters you've filled in to find the title and author of the book Dewey just finished reading.

Illustration: Scott Peck

Answer on page 50

Hint on page 47

$8 + 3 =$ _____

$18 ÷ 2 =$ _____

$2 × 2 =$ _____

$21 - 2 =$ _____

$9 × 2 =$ _____

$4 × 2 =$ _____

$31 - 6 =$ _____

$7 + 6 =$ _____

$25 ÷ 5 =$ _____

$23 - 4 =$ _____

$8 - 6 =$ _____

$5 × 5 =$ _____

$4 × 4 =$ _____

$19 ÷ 19 =$ _____

$30 - 10 =$ _____

$2 × 10 =$ _____

$27 ÷ 3 =$ _____

$9 - 6 =$ _____

$6 ÷ 6 =$ _____

$7 + 4 =$ _____

$15 ÷ 3 =$ _____

COLOR BY NUMBERS

Use the key to color the spaces and you'll find something that might bug you.

Illustration: Rob Sepanak

KEY

1 dot—Yellow   4 dots—Light Green
2 dots—Dark Green   5 dots—Brown
3 dots—Black   6 dots—Blue

Answer on page 50

PET PERCENTAGES

Swineton Elementary School conducted a pet survey. It's up to you to use the

Hint on page 47

QUESTIONS

1. What percentage of students have at least one pet? _____
2. What percentage of students have no pets?
3. What percentage of students have dogs? _____
4. What percentage of students have cats? _____
5. What percentage of students have fish? _____
6. What percentage of students have frogs? _____
7. What percentage of students have fish or frogs? _____
8. What percentage of students have a dog or a cat? _____
9. What's the most popular pet?
10. How many students have a pet with four legs? _____

Answer on page 51

findings to answer
the school newspaper
reporter's questions.

SURVEY FINDINGS

25% of students have only dogs.
23% of students have only cats.
9% of students have cats and fish.
11% of students have dogs and fish.
13% of students have only hamsters.
8% of students have hamsters and fish.
3% of students have hamsters and frogs.
1% of students have only frogs.
The remaining students have no pets.

Illustration: Rocky Fuller

GOOD BUY?

Marty used the money he had saved to buy a baseball card for $30. A few weeks later, he sold the card to a baseball-card store for $40. The store had it on sale for $50 when Marty found out it was worth more. He bought the card back for $50 and then sold it to another collector for $60. In the end, did he make a profit, or did he lose money?

Answer on page 51

TEAM

BASEBALL = LIFE

COOPERSTOWN

0 0 0 0

CARDS

Hint on page 47

Illustration: David Helton

IN THE BAG

Charlene is at the recycling center. Each black bag contains 50 glass bottles. Each white bag contains 50 aluminum cans. How much money should she receive for all she's brought in?

Paper	$.20 a pound
Bottles	$.10 each
Aluminum	$.05 each
Scrap metal	$.35 a pound

Illustration: Jerry Zimmerman

Answer on page 51

RITA'S RESERVATIONS

Rita's Rest is a bed-and-breakfast. Can you look at Rita's calendar and help her schedule the reservation dates for the

people listed? None of these guests will stay on the same night. You can pencil in the names right on the calendar.

Hint on page 47

AUGUST

SUNDAY	MONDAY	TUESDAY	WEDNESDAY	THURSDAY	FRIDAY	SATURDAY
1 FULL	2 Nature Hike	3	4 FULL	5 Campfire by Lake	6 Art Show FULL	7 FULL
8	9	10 Strawberry Festival	11	12 Cookout FULL	13 Antique Car Show	14
15 FULL	16 Dog Show	17 Summer Fest FULL	18 FULL	19 FULL	20	21
22	23 Relatives Visit FULL	24 FULL	25	26 Outdoor FULL	27 Concert FULL	28 Boat Parade
29	30 FULL	31				

Mr. and Mrs. Barker can come anytime for one night. They love dogs and are bringing two.

The Swimma family wants to come after the 21st for two days.

Mr. and Mrs. Varoom want to come for the car show and would like to stay for two days if possible.

The Sunny family wants to come for four days in a row.

Mr. and Mrs. Pal want to come on a Friday and stay through Sunday.

Illustration: Rick Geary

Answer on page 51

OCTA GONE

Place each of the numbers from 1 to 9 into one of the octagons so that the number in each square is the sum of the numbers in the four octagons that surround it. The numbers 4 and 8 have already been positioned for you. When all the numbers are in the proper octagons, look for the numbers beneath the blanks in our riddle. The letter in the octagon goes in the blank with the matching number.

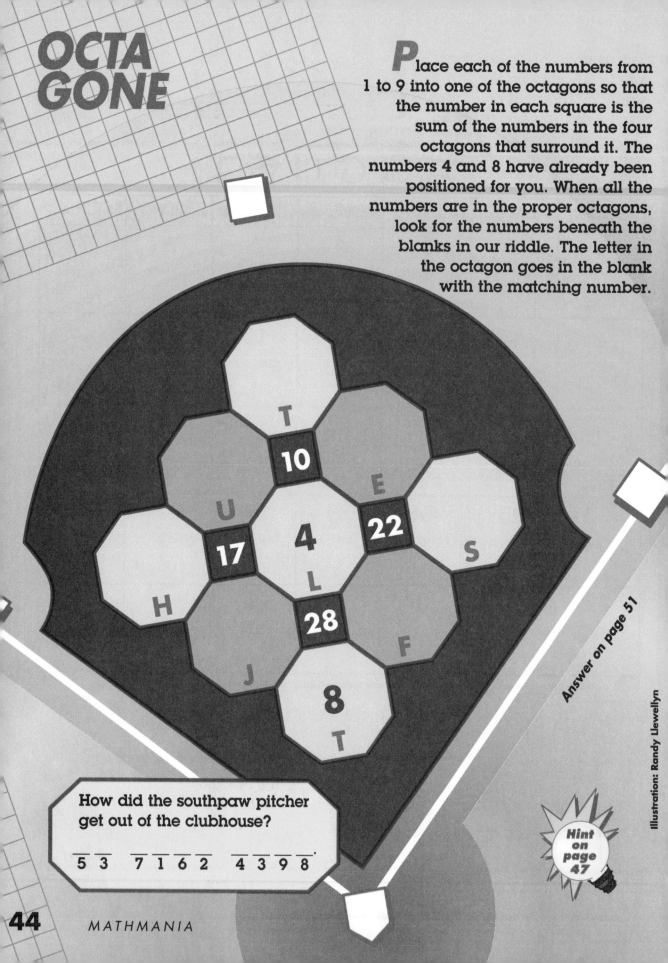

T

10

E

U

22

17

4

S

L

H

28

F

J

8

T

Answer on page 51

Illustration: Randy Llewellyn

How did the southpaw pitcher get out of the clubhouse?

$\overline{5}$ $\overline{3}$ $\overline{7}$ $\overline{1}$ $\overline{6}$ $\overline{2}$ $\overline{4}$ $\overline{3}$ $\overline{9}$ $\overline{8}$.

Hint on page 47

FOLLOW FRACTIONS

Connect the fractions starting from the smallest to the largest to get through this maze.

$$\frac{9}{10}$$

$$\frac{4}{5}$$

$$\frac{3}{4}$$

$$\frac{15}{16}$$

FINISH

$$\frac{1}{8}$$

$$\frac{7}{10}$$

$$\frac{1}{16}$$

START

$$\frac{1}{4}$$

$$\frac{1}{2}$$

Answer on page 51

HINTS AND BRIGHT IDEAS

*T*hese hints may help with some of the trickier puzzles.

COVER
There are no more than 9 and no fewer than 5 of either type of animal.

THREE LITTLE PIGS (page 3)
What is the lowest number that can be evenly divided by 2, 3, and 4?

PIÑATA PUZZLER (page 7)
Think about when each person was supposed to get a turn. That will help you figure out how many children didn't get a swing.

A FISH TALE (pages 8-9)
The bowl for the youngest fish has three fish in it.

ALL NEW DEPTHS (pages 12-13)
Remember that to match our answer, all the numbers will be used at least once. It might help you to figure out all the answers first, and then look for them in the grid.

RIVER RUN (page 14)
Divide the total distance of each river by the number of miles per hour the kayaker can paddle.

DOMINO THEORY (pages 16-17)
Use all 28 possible number combinations. Cross off each domino as you find a place for it. Put tile halves with the same number next to each other. When a tile with the same number of dots on each side is placed crosswise, the dots on the dominoes on either side should be the same. For instance, check the 3-3 domino that's given. Remember that dominoes can be flipped around, so you can place either side against another domino. For example, 2-3 is the number pair for one tile. That domino can be placed against either a 2 or a 3.

DIGIT DOES IT (pages 18-19)
The word *Inspector* appears in the note's greeting. Use the code numbers from this word to help figure out the rest of the message.

TILE TOTAL (page 20)

How large is the area Kathy wants to tile? Multiply 2 × 4 to get the total number of square feet. There are 12 inches in a foot. 9 tiles of the size she's considering will fill 1 square foot.

MARKET PICKS (page 21)

A quick way to get started is to look at the digits in the ones place (the last one on the right). Which four digits will equal 2, the digit in the ones place of $11.22?

NUMBER NOODLER (page 24)

Use clues 1, 4, and 5 to narrow the choices down to a small set of numbers. Then use the other clues to finish the job.

CROSSWORD RIDDLE (pages 26-27)

Ay is "yes." *Fe* and *wt.* are two other answers that ye may find helpful.

MYSTERIOUS MINUTES (pages 30-31)

Figure out the time each singer or musician spent practicing. Whoever took the sandwich had to be free at 7:00 p.m.

LIBRARY LAUGHS (page 36)

Remember to consult the books to find the letter that matches each number.

PET PERCENTAGES (pages 38-39)

Don't worry about how many students are represented in each percentage. Just focus on the percentages themselves.

GOOD BUY? (page 40)

Add up the prices Marty paid for the card. Now add up the prices he sold it for.

RITA'S RESERVATIONS (pages 42-43)

None of the new guests can stay on days that are already marked *FULL*.

OCTA GONE (page 44)

5 goes in the octagon farthest to the left.

ANSWERS

ZIP IT (page 10)

89212—7   66804—1, 2, 6, 8
33021—3, 5   43666—4, 9, 10

DOTS A LOT (page 11)

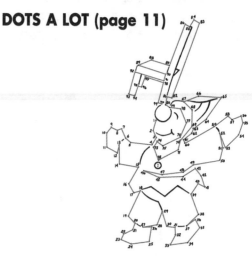

COVER

Clem counted 8 cows and 6 chickens.

THREE LITTLE PIGS (page 3)

They will all meet again in 12 days. 12 is the lowest common denominator of 2, 3, and 4.

ALOHA! (pages 4-5)

$1 = 2 \div 2$ $5 = 10 \div 2$ $9 = 11 - 2$
$2 = 0 + 2$ $6 = 2 \times 3$ $10 = (2 \times 2) \times 2 + 2$
$3 = 1 + 2$ $7 = 5 + 2$ $11 = 22 \div 2$
$4 = 2 \times 2$ $8 = (2 \times 2) \times 2$ $12 = (2 \times 2) \times (2 + 1)$

STACKING STANLEY (page 6)

PIÑATA PUZZLER (page 7)

7 children got a turn (Ariel, Courtney, Eleanor, Francisco, Geraldo, Herman, and Ignacio), and 4 didn't (Brett, Darrice, Jamie, and Kiandra).

A FISH TALE (pages 8-9)

UP TO 6 MONTHS OLD	6 MONTHS TO 1 YEAR OLD	OLDER THAN 1 YEAR
Tiny	Spot	Goldy
Finley	Blubber	Ray
Big Red	Aqua	Zeebee
	Pesce	

ALL NEW DEPTHS (pages 12-13)

LAKE	DEPTH
Baykal	$5000 + 300 + 10 + 5 = 5315$
Tanganyika	$4000 + 800 + 20 + 3 = 4823$
Caspian Sea	$3000 + 300 + 60 + 3 = 3363$
Issyk Kul	$2000 + 300 + 3 = 2303$
Nyasa	$2000 + 200 + 80 = 2280$
Great Slave	$2000 + 10 + 5 = 2015$
Great Bear	$1000 + 400 + 60 + 3 = 1463$
Superior	$1000 + 300 + 30 = 1330$
Michigan	$900 + 20 + 3 = 923$
Titicaca	$900 + 20 + 2 = 922$
Ontario	$800 + 2 = 802$
Huron	$700 + 50 = 750$
Ladoga	$700 + 30 + 8 = 738$
Reindeer	$700 + 20 = 720$
Athabasca	$400 + 7 = 407$
Kariba	$300 + 90 = 390$
Aral Sea	$200 + 20 = 220$
Erie	$200 + 10 = 210$
Maracaibo	$100 + 10 + 5 = 115$
Balkhash	$80 + 5 = 85$

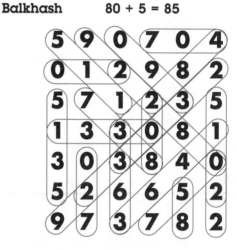

RIVER RUN (page 14)

Qan will arrive first in 3 hours
  (24 ÷ 8 = 3).
Pablo will arrive second in 4 hours
  (44 ÷ 11 = 4).
Olivia will arrive third in 5 hours
  (30 ÷ 6 = 5).
Noel will arrive fourth in 6 hours
  (42 ÷ 7 = 6).

FAMOUS NAME (page 15)

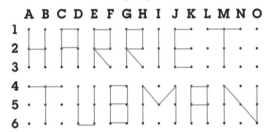

DOMINO THEORY (pages 16-17)

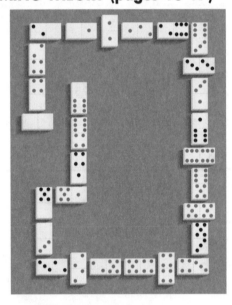

DIGIT DOES IT (pages 18-19)

Dear Inspector Digit,
Aw, shucks! This sounds corny, but
I should have listened when I was in the
crib. My pop said to keep my ears open and
stay away from crime. It's time to cash in
my chips and wish myself into the cornfield.
Good luck cleaning out all 21 ears!
Rob Cobb

a-5	f-14	l-20	r-7	w-13
b-15	g-2	m-17	s-16	y-4
c-18	h-9	n-1	t-12	
d-10	i-22	o-21	u-19	
e-8	k-3	p-11	v-6	

TILE TOTAL (page 20)

Kathy should choose the box with 72 tiles.
She needs 8 square feet of tiles (2 × 4).
Each square foot requires 9 tiles (9 × 8 = 72).

MARKET PICKS (page 21)

Dana bought the soap, vitamins,
bottled water, and box of tissues
($2.29 + $5.64 + $1.40 + $1.89 = $11.22).

SCRAMBLED PICTURE (pages 22-23)

NUMBER NOODLER (page 24)

37
From Clues 1 and 5: not larger than 50,
    but not smaller than 20
From Clue 4: either 31, 33, 35, 37, or 39
From Clue 2: not 33
From Clue 3: not 35
From Clue 6: not 31
From Clue 7: not 39

ROVER (page 25)

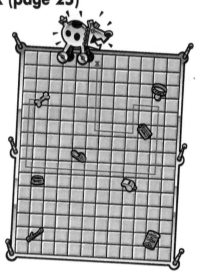

CROSSWORD RIDDLE (pages 26-27)

They always make your day:
TWENTY-FOUR HOURS.

SURE SHOTS (page 28)
Jessica made 8 baskets.
12 × 5 = 60 (no misses)
11 × 5 = 55 – 2 = 53
10 × 5 = 50 – 4 = 46
9 × 5 = 45 – 6 = 39
8 × 5 = 40 – 8 = 32
8 × 5 = 40 (points); 4 × 2 = 8 (points off);
40 – 8 = 32

BRAINTEASER (page 29)
A is the higher total (15). Remember that
anything times 0 equals 0.

MYSTERIOUS MINUTES (pages 30-31)
Only Bill Frogg had the time to eat
    the sandwich.
Ali was out of the room only from
    7:00 to 7:09.
L. E. Fant and Anna Conda started at 6:30.
    Their 4 songs took 11 minutes each
    (4 × 11 = 44 minutes). They finished
    at 7:14.
Ty started practicing at 6:49. He finished
    at 7:09.
Robyn practiced for 44 + 6 (15 – 9) =
    50 minutes; 6:39 + 50 minutes = 7:29.
Bill finished at 6:59 (7:29 – 30 minutes).
    He had the time!

MATHMAGIC (page 32)
"There are no *orange kangaroos* in *Denmark*!"
There are a few combinations that would
work, but those are the words most people
would think of.

PRECISE ICE (page 33)

TOUCHDOWN TIME (pages 34-35)
The Hornets scored only on their 3rd try. The
Sharks scored on their 2nd and 3rd attempts.

LIBRARY LAUGHS (page 36)

8 + 3 = 11	K	8 – 6 = 2	B
18 ÷ 2 = 9	I	5 × 5 = 25	Y
2 × 2 = 4	D	4 × 4 = 16	P
21 – 2 = 19	S	19 ÷ 19 = 1	A
9 × 2 = 18	R	30 – 10 = 20	T
4 × 2 = 8	H	2 × 10 = 20	T
31 – 6 = 25	Y	27 ÷ 3 = 9	I
7 + 6 = 13	M	9 – 6 = 3	C
25 ÷ 5 = 5	E	6 ÷ 6 = 1	A
23 – 4 = 19	S	7 + 4 = 11	K
		15 ÷ 3 = 5	E

KIDS RHYMES
by Patti Cake

COLOR BY NUMBERS (page 37)